Boosting your Business Profitability

Toye Adelaja

INTRODUCTION

Improving a business profit involves looking at the ways of increasing sales revenue and reducing cost. Profitability is very paramount to a reasonable existence of every business organization. The main motive of every business is to make a continuous profit.

Any business that is characterized by losses is very vulnerable to liquidation. As a result of this, maximization of profit and minimization of cost should be given priority in every profit-oriented business.

Table of Contents

CHAPTER 1

1.1. What is profit?

Profit can be specifically divided into two; namely gross profit and Net profit

1.1.1. Gross Profit

How to determine a gross profit or a gross Loss? When revenue is greater than the cost of the goods sold, we have a gross profit but if otherwise, we have a gross loss. The revenue is the value at which goods are sold. Revenue is the value of sales.

The cost of goods sold for a retailer is the cost of goods in its beginning inventory plus the cost of goods purchased minus the cost of its ending inventory plus the cost of putting goods in a saleable condition. Costs such as purchase cost, carriage inward, costs of renovating or repair of the product are classified as part of a cost of the goods when added together. Trading account is prepared to get gross profit or loss.

Look at the following illustration

Calculate the gross profit or the gross loss for each of the following entity:

Names	Revenue	Cost of Goods Sold	Gross Profits /Loss
X	$15,000	$15,050	- $50
Y	$ 6,500	$5,600	$900
Z	$10,300	$9,560	$740

Explanations:

Negative figure signify loss while positive figures denote profit. It means that company X makes a gross loss of $50 while both companies Y and Z earn gross profits of $900 and $740 respectively.

1.1.2. NET PROFIT

Net Profit in the income statement (profit and loss accounts) is the gross profit plus other income such as commission received, rent received etc less other expenses such as salary, rent paid, repair and maintenance of machinery, advertisement etc. Where the total income is higher than the total expenses, we say there is a net profit but if otherwise, there is a net loss. Statement of income or profit and loss account is prepared to determine net profit or net loss.

CHAPTER 2

2.1. Increasing Revenue

One of the ways of increasing a business profit is by increasing revenue. Revenue can also be referred to as sales. It is measured by multiplying the number of units of goods sold by the selling price per unit. Example; 5 bags of rice are sold at $45 each, the total revenue from the sales is 5× $45 = $225.

There are different strategies to increase your sales. The following are some strategies for increasing sales:

2.1. 1. Invite, win and retain customers

How can you win customers and retain them for life?

The followings are the ways to win and retain customers for life:

A business that wants to make a continuous profit must not be losing customers to competitors. A business that desires to be successful must keep their customers coming back by satisfying them.

What must a business do to establish a reputation for its services? Inasmuch as customers are the final judges of qualities of services of a business, the satisfactions of customers should be given pre-eminent. The right thing to do is to ask customers what specific aspects of services are most important to them. Extensive research has been done in this area.

Here are the most important ingredients for providing the kinds of services that keep customers coming back:

BE ATTRACTIVE

Customers are attracted by a well packaged and neat product. Appearance can be deceptive, but customers draw a lot of conclusions about the qualities of services on the basis of what they see. For example, a drug that is stained or dirty will be repulsive to customers, irrespective of its efficacy. Anything customers see, feel, touch, hear, or smell concerning your business is shaping their opinion of your service for better or worse.

You must be looking at your business through your customers' eyes, and make the effort to put forth a first-class image. This is not a frivolous expense.

BE RELIABLE

Consistent Performances are what customers want most. More than anything else, they want services that they can depend on. More specifically these mean:

Do what you say you are going to do
Do it right the first time
Get it done speedily.

Example of reliability and consistency are mentioned below:

A fanatical commitment to reliability is the key reason that federal Express has established itself as the premier company in the overnight delivery business. It is committed to the goal of "no service failures," which means delivering all packages by 10:30 the next morning. While it may not be perfect, its track record is nothing short of outstanding.

BE RESPONSIVE

Being responsive means keeping customers informed and providing the service as soon as possible. It also means being accessible, available, and willing to help customers whenever they have problems.

Timely responsiveness can keep customers and even win customers. Like it or not, we live in an era of instant everything. When customers want services, they want them now. In a Hotel grill in Hungary, each table is equipped with a ten-minute hour glass. If your order isn't taken in ten minutes, the meal is free. The Hotel exhibits responsiveness so that it can keep customers coming back.

BE CREDIBLE

One thing customers like to pay for is peace of mind. Customers will definitely revisit the business that has their interest at heart. Customers want security, integrity, and the assurance that if there is a problem, it will be immediately attended to without extra costs. They do not want deception and extra charges. If they buy a product, they want it to be free from doubt and danger.

In conclusion, customers should be treated like kings in business. As a business professional, you have to be careful in handling your customers if you don't want to lose them. You must try as much as possible to provide 100% quality of service to your customers.

For example, a business that has 200 customers and providing 95% quality of service and 5% failure delivery may lose some customers. The business will lose 10 current customers (5% ×200), and 100 customers in total (10 ×10) if 1 customer that is dissatisfied with the service of the business discourage 10 people that want to patronize the business.

2.1.2. Increasing your selling skills

Every business organization derives its income from either sales of products or sales of services. Without income, no business can be successful, and without sales, income cannot be generated. Sales are very important in every business entity. It needs to be given special attention.
Are you an entrepreneur or sales representative? You need to intensify your selling ability. Here are the ways in which you can increase your selling skills:

1) Learn how to speak in public places

You need to learn how to face the crowd and convince them about your products and services. When you are in the public, you must be bold enough to introduce your products or services to the members of the public.

2) Study your key competitors

Study your competitors and discover what they do differently. Watch how they attract and retain potential customers. Try to search for your competitors' websites. Attend their trade exhibition and find out how they win customers and keep them for life. You should be able to adopt their methods in a better way so that many of their customers will start to patronize you. This kind of method can improve your selling skills and boost your sales.

3) Increase your online attendance.

You need to improve on the frequency in which you visit the internet. Create your own website and invite prospective customers through it. You need to post interesting content on the website to attract clients.

4) Record every conversation between you and your clients.

Play and replay the conversation to know your performances. Find out whether your response was okay or not and look for ways of improving it during the next conversation.

5) Get out of your comfort zone

If you want to improve your selling skills, you need to move out of your comfort zone. Tastes of customers are changing as technology is changing. If you have been using the same technique for a long period, you need to change to a new one that supersedes the former technique of sales. You must not be complacent with old things. Get new materials about selling. Update yourself by attending seminars.

6) Think in the same way as your customers

Learn how to think in the same way as your customers think. You need to observe how your customers behave. You also have to know what your customers want, need and like.

7) Develop your sales process

A sale process is the whole activities involved in selling. It starts from the time you make initial contact and ends at the time you actually sell your products or services. A Sales process that is appropriate in one business may not work for another one. Sales process depends on the peculiarity of each organization.

2.1.3. Review all your Prices

Do you quote or charge the same prices for all customers? Some customers are less price sensitive than others, especially if they are not paying the bills themselves. When entities such as government and large organizations are paying bills on behalf of your customers, you may increase your prices because the customers will be less sensitive to the price increase.

CHAPTER 3

Reducing Costs

3.1. Costs can be divided into two main types. They are direct costs and indirect costs.

3.1.1. Direct Costs

Direct costs are the costs that can be traced to the production or sales of a particular unit of a product. Direct costs can be sub-divided into direct costs of production and direct costs of sales.

1. Direct Costs of production are the costs that can be identified with the production of a particular unit of an output or service. Examples of direct costs are as follows:

- Costs of raw materials used for production
- Wages paid to factory workers for work that is directly related to production
- Expenses incurred directly for a specific project or a job.

2. Direct Costs of sales are the costs that can be traced and identified with a unit of goods sold or service rendered. Examples of the direct cost of sales are wages paid to sales representatives and carriage inward of goods.

3.1.2. Indirect Costs

Indirect costs can be classified into the indirect costs of production and indirect cost of sales.

Indirect costs of production: These are the cost that cannot be traced to the production of a particular unit of an output or service. All material, labor costs and expense which cannot be identified as direct costs are termed indirect costs. The indirect material costs, indirect labor costs and indirect factory expenses which are the three elements of indirect costs of production are collectively known as overheads.

The indirect cost of sales: These are the costs that cannot be traced to the sales of a particular unit of goods. Examples of the indirect costs of sales are rent of office premises, salaries, office expenses. The summation of these indirect costs of sales is equal to overhead costs.

Having identified the types of costs, the next thing is to find ways of reducing these costs.

How to Reduce Direct Costs

The following are the procedures to reduce either direct cost of production or direct cost of sales:

i. Look for credible and reliable suppliers that sell quality goods at cheaper prices.

ii. Take cash discounts from suppliers by not delaying the payment. Many suppliers give cash discounts or rebate to buyers that pay for goods purchased within the stipulated time on the agreement of sales. This is better than borrowing money to purchase goods.

iii. Negotiate for a cheaper and reasonable carriage inward cost.

iv. Pay reasonable and cheap labor cost.

How to Reduce Business Overhead Costs

It is very important to know the meaning of overhead cost before we talk about how to reduce it. Overhead cost is a cost that cannot be identified with the production of a particular unit of an item. It can also be defined as a cost that cannot be linked to a specific service. Examples of overhead costs are fuel and lubricant expenses, rent, electricity bill, water expenses, phone and internet expenses etc.

It is very imperative and essential for business owners to reduce overhead costs and still maintaining prudence in this age of economically unstable environment. The following are some ways of reducing overhead cost:

1) Reduce Your Office Rent

You can reduce your rent by relocating to a cheaper office. Ensure that customers' patronages are not adversely affected if you move to a new location. Instead of spending money on renting offices, you can resort to working from home as well.

2) Reduce your electricity bill

Installation of energy-saving high fixtures could reduce your electricity bill. You must also ensure that bulbs inside your offices and office premises are switched off during the day when the sun is still shining enough to bring light. Ensure that machines and equipment that are not in use are not running unnecessarily.

3) Switch your phone to VOIP

If you want your phone bill to be reduced, you can resort to skype, Tango or google voice. The VOIP is less expensive than mobile and land line.

4) Reduce paper consumption

Have you been communicating through the posting of letters? You can reduce paper usage by sending and receiving information through emails. If you compare the cost of papers and postages to cost of internet subscription, you will discover that the cost of internet subscription is cheaper.

5) Reduce Salary wisely

Is it advisable to reduce salary? Reduction of salary can only be recommended where an employee is not productive. If you discover that some employees are redundant, you can decrease their salaries or terminate their appointment where there is no improvement on their own part.

6) Engage the Service of Outsourcing Accountant.

At the initial stage of your business, you can engage the service of an outsourcing accountant. The cost is relatively cheaper when you compare it with the salary you will be paying to a permanent accountant.

7) Engage the Service of a professional Accountant

Professional Accountants are experts. They know when best to reduce overhead costs. Do not hesitate to consult them. Don't mind the costs; you will definitely see the positive impact of their services on your business.

In conclusion, reduction of overhead costs can lead to an increase in profit. Don't focus on the reduction of cost alone. Consider both negative and positive result it will have on the profit and on the business as a whole.

CHAPTER 4

Prioritize Profitability

You need to arrange your products and services in order of the level of profitability. Resources are not sufficient to achieve all your goals. You cannot invest in every viable product or service because of limited resources. You have to invest your funds in those products and services that have higher profits and higher turnover rates. If this is done, your profit will be maximized.

How do you know those products that have higher turnover rate? A stock turnover rate is a financial ratio that is used to test the velocity at which goods are being sold and replaced.

The formula for calculating stock turnover rate is:

$$\text{Stock turnover rate} = \frac{\text{Cost of Sales}}{\text{Average inventory}}$$

The following information is used as an example:

Products	Cost of sales	Revenue	Gross Profit	Opening inventory	Closing inventory
A	$600	$1,000	$400	20	20
B	$800	$1,200	$400	10	20
C	$250	$650	$400	50	15
D	$450	$850	$400	50	45
E	$780	$900	$120	30	80

Stock turnover for each product is as follows:

Stock turnover for A

$$= \frac{600}{(20+20)/2}$$

= 30times

Stock turnover for B

$$= \frac{800}{(10+20)/2}$$

= 53 times

Stock turnover for C

$$= \frac{250}{(50+15)/2}$$

= 7.69

= 8 times

Stock Turnover for D

$$= \frac{450}{(50+45)/2}$$

= 9.47

= 10 times

From the table above, it is discovered that products A, B, C, and D have the same gross profits.
Ranking of products according to stock turn- over rate

Products	Stock turnover rate
B	53
A	30
D	10
C	8

Notes:

Where products that have highest gross profits are having the same level of gross profit, the products should be prioritized using stock turnover rate ratio.

In conclusion, the resources of the company should be invested on the products above according to the ranking.

CHAPTER 5

Establish Effective Internal Control System

Audit operational standard (guideline) defines internal control as being:

The whole system of control, financial and otherwise established by the management of an enterprise in order to carry on the business of an enterprise in an orderly and efficient manner, ensure adherence to management policies, safeguard the assets and secure as far as possible the completeness and accuracy of records.

Internal controls are procedures which ensure that all transactions, assets, and liabilities are recorded correctly.

The following are the objectives of internal control:

- Carrying on the business of the company in an orderly and efficient manner

- To ensure adherence to management policies

- To safeguard assets

- To ensure completeness and accuracy of records

There are some conditions that must be met before internal control system can function effectively. The following conditions must be put in place for effective internal control system:

1. Management should not override the laid-down control.

2. Internal control must be documented for future reference.

3. The objective of internal control must be communicated to all members of staff.

4. Personnel in charge of the company's transactions should have adequate training, experience, proficiency and be well motivated.

5. There should be a clearly defined organizational structure showing the segregation of duties.

6. The Internal control system should not be too complex. It should be simple and flexible.

It should be noted and emphasized that the main purpose of internal control is to prevent waste, errors, fraud and embezzlement.

Internal control prevents theft, losses of money and mismanagement.

Component of internal control are as follows:

- Physical control
- Authorization / Approval Control
- Personnel Control
- Arithmetic and Accounting Control
- Management Control
- Supervisory Control
- Segregation of duty
- Acknowledgment of performance

Physical Control

Assets must be physically kept secured. Examples of assets are machinery, motor vehicle, inventory and cash. They should be physically secured and maintained.

Authorization and Approval

All transactions should require authorization or approval of an appropriate responsible person. The limits of these authorizations should be specified.

Arithmetic and Accounting Control

All transactions must be recorded and calculated correctly. Errors and mistakes should be avoided all the time. There are some ways that can be adopted to ensure arithmetic and accounting control. They are the preparation of trial balance, control accounts, and bank reconciliation.

Personnel Control

There should be procedures to ensure that personnel has capabilities commensurate with their responsibilities. It is generally believed that proper functioning of any system depends on the competence and integrity of those operating it. The qualification, selection, and training of personnel involved, are important criteria to be considered in setting up any internal control system.

Management Control

Management controls are outside the routine control system. These may include the establishment of internal audit department or the use of managerial accounts to control operations.

Supervisory Control

These are controls exercised by high- level management or their subordinates. They are designed to ensure that the company is operating as intended.

Segregation of Duties

Segregation of duties ensures that not one person is responsible for all aspects of transactions from the beginning to the end. This is fundamental to a good internal control system. The involvement of different members of staff in a client operation minimizes the risk of mistakes and deliberate fraud.

Acknowledgment of performance

There should be a set of procedures designed which ensures that everybody performing a duty or a function acknowledges his or her activity by means of signature and names.

If the internal control system is effectively implemented, cost, fraud, theft, and mismanagement of fund will be reduced, and hence profit will be increased.

CHAPTER 6

USE OF INVENTORY CONTROL TO BOOST PROFIT

Inventory control is a system whereby a business entity ensures that excessive inventory is not held and inadequate inventory is not kept.

Objectives of inventory control are as follows:

1. To maintain a large size of inventory for efficient and smooth production and sales operations

2. To maintain a minimum investment in stock to maximize profitability

It is the objective of every business entity to boost profit. Inventory should be well managed if this objective is to be achieved. If adequate inventory is held, customers' demand will be satisfied and hence keep them coming. If excessive inventory is held, too much fund that should have been invested in other profitable business will be tied down in the inventory.

In a nutshell, effective inventory control and management should:

1. Ensure continuous supply of raw materials to facilitate uninterrupted productions.

2. Maintain sufficient stocks of raw materials in time of scarce supply and anticipate price changes

3. Maintain sufficient finished goods inventory for smooth sales operation and efficient customer service

4. Control the investment in inventories and keep it at an optimum level.

Inventory Management Techniques

To manage inventories efficiently and effectively, solutions must be provided to the following:

How much should be ordered?

This is the process of determining the appropriate quantity to be ordered. This is the economy order quantity (EOQ).

When should it be ordered?

This relates to the problem of determining the re-order point in order to bridge the gap of any uncertainty of supply.

Economic Order Quantity (EOQ)

This is the inventory level which minimizes the total ordering and carrying costs. It is the optimum inventory size that minimizes the total ordering and holding costs of inventory.

There are many methods of determining economic Order Quantity (EOQ). They are the formula method, trial and error method, and graphical method. The formula method will be discussed here.

Ordering Costs: Ordering costs are used in case of raw materials (or supplies) and include costs incurred in the following areas: the cost of requisition, purchase ordering costs, transporting costs (carriage inward), receiving costs and inspecting costs.

Carrying or Holding Costs: These are the costs incurred for maintaining, preserving and storing inventory. These costs include storage (warehousing costs, stores handling costs and clerical staff cost) deterioration, obsolescence and insurance

$$EOQ = \sqrt{2DCo/Cc}$$

Interpretation of the formula

D = Annual quantity demanded
Co = Ordering cost per order
Cc = carrying cost per unit

The following illustration is used as an example.

The following information was extracted from the book of Samothex Company, a dealer of wheat.

Annual demand   1,000,000 bags of wheat
Annual cost to carry 10%
Cost to place orders $25
Cost per unit $2,000

You are required to calculate Economic Order Quantity.

SOLUTION

$EOQ = \sqrt{2DCo/Cc}$
$= \sqrt{2 \times 1,000,000 \times 25 / 2,000 \times 10\%}$
$= \sqrt{50,000,000/200}$
$= 500$

The Economic Order Quantity is 500 bags of wheat.

500 bags of wheat should be ordered each time order is being made to minimize all the inventory costs. The economic Order Quantity answered the question of how much to order.

Re-order point

Re-order point is the inventory level at which an order should be placed to replenish inventory. It can also be defined as the level at which you should order more products to prevent shortages.

The formula for calculating reorder point when there is no fluctuation in the usage and lead time (that is, under certainty), is lead time multiplied by average usage.

Lead time is the period between the time an order is made and the time it arrives.

The following information can be used to calculate Re-order Point:

Assuming that the economic order quantity is 600units and average usage is 60units per week.

Calculate the reorder point when the lead time is 3 weeks.

Solution

Reorder point = Lead time × Average Usage

$$= 3 \times 60$$

$$= 180 \text{ units}$$

The Order should be placed for replenishment immediately the stock level reaches 180 units.

REFERENCES

Michael LeBoeuf, Ph. D. How to win Customers and Keep Them for   Life (Berkley Publishing Group,375 , New York)

ICAN Study Pack (Strategic Financial Management) 2009

Emile Woolf (1979) Auditing Today (Third Edition) Prentice Hall international (UK) Ltd

www.accountinghour.com